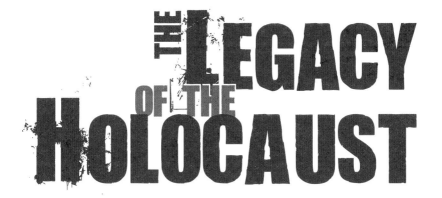

by Jason Skog

Content Adviser:
Harold Marcuse, PhD, Associate Professor,
Department of History, University of California, Santa Barbara

Reading Adviser:
Alexa Sandmann, EdD,
Professor of Literacy, College and Graduate School
of Education, Health, and Human Services, Kent State University

COMPASS POINT BOOKS
a capstone imprint

Compass Point Books
1710 Roe Crest Drive
North Mankato, MN 56003

Editor: Brenda Haugen
Designer: Ashlee Suker
Media Researcher: Svetlana Zhurkin
Library Consultant: Kathleen Baxter
Production Specialist: Sarah Bennett
Cartographer: XNR Productions, Inc.

On the Cover
The Hall of Names at Yad Vashem, Israel's official memorial to Jewish victims
of the Holocaust

Image Credits
Alamy/Jon Arnold Images, 50; AP Photo/Jacquelyn Martin, 16; Courtesy of the Leo Baeck
Institute, New York, 18; Digital Stock, 59; DVIC/NARA, 10, 58 (top); Getty Images:
Hulton Archive/Keystone, 30, Hulton Archive/Keystone/Fred Ramage, 54, Uriel Sinai,
cover, 49; Library of Congress, 22, 27, 32; Newscom: 20, 45, AFP, 47, AFP/Dimitar
Dilkoff, 41, AFP/Interpress/Igor Potemkin, 46, AFP/Stan Honda, 38, 40, AFP/Tang
Chhin Sothy, 43, SIPA/GOESS, 36; Shutterstock/Sascha Hahn, 56, 58 (bottom); United
States Holocaust Memorial Museum: 19, 52, courtesy of Lee T. Stinchfield, 5, courtesy of
Lewis Shabasson, 13, courtesy of Martin Silver, 25, courtesy of Morris and Lala Fishman,
14, courtesy of William and Dorothy McLaughlin, 34, Israel Government Press Office, 37,
National Archives and Records Administration, 9, 28, 33, National Archives and Records
Administration, AP Photo, 11, National Archives and Records Administration, Ministere des
Anciens Combattants et Victimes de Guerre, 6.

Library of Congress Cataloging-in-Publication Data
Skog, Jason.
  The legacy of the Holocaust / by Jason Skog.
     p. cm.—(The Holocaust)
  Includes bibliographical references and index.
  ISBN 978-0-7565-4393-8 (library binding)
  ISBN 978-0-7565-4444-7 (paperback)
  1. Holocaust, Jewish (1939–1945)—Juvenile literature. 2. Holocaust,
Jewish (1939–1945)—Influence—Juvenile literature. I. Title. II. Series.
  D804.34.S57 2011
  940.53'1814—dc22   2010026494

Visit Compass Point Books on the Internet at www.capstonepub.com

Printed in the United States of America in Stevens Point, Wisconsin.
012012
006551R

Table of Contents

Preface

In 1933 an Austrian-born politician named Adolf Hitler became the chancellor of Germany. Hitler was the leader of the National Socialist German Workers Party—the Nazi Party. Hitler was bitterly anti-Semitic and blamed the Jews for Germany's economic problems.

Hitler dreamed of populating Europe with Aryans, members of what he called a master race. The Aryans included Germans with fair skin, blond hair, and blue eyes. Hitler believed Jews were the enemy of the Aryans, and he developed a plan to isolate and kill them. Hitler called his plan the Final Solution of the Jewish Question.

With Hitler in power, life for Jewish people in Germany became increasingly difficult and dangerous. By the mid-1930s, Jewish businesses were boycotted and vandalized. Jewish Germans were forced to identify themselves by wearing the Star of David on their clothing. Jewish children were expelled from German schools. Jews were forced to leave their homes and live in certain areas, apart from Aryans, and they lost their German citizenship. Hitler's police beat and killed some Jews on the streets.

The Nazis sent millions of Jews to concentration camps in many parts of Europe. Some camps were killing centers; others were prison and forced-labor camps. Prisoners were beaten and subjected to painful experiments in which they could be maimed or killed. Survival was rare. Prisoners who were not killed in the gas chambers or shot by guards often died of starvation or illness. Besides Jews, the camps held political prisoners, homosexuals, Jehovah's Witnesses, disabled people, and people who were called gypsies.

Hitler's troops invaded Austria, Czechoslovakia, and Poland, and France and Great Britain declared war on Germany September 3, 1939. World War II became a fight between the Allies—led by France, Great Britain, the United States, and the Soviet Union—and the Axis powers of Germany, Italy, and Japan.

Until their defeat in 1945, the Nazis killed 11 million people in more than a dozen countries. Six million were Jews—two-thirds of the Jewish population in Europe. More than a million Jewish children were killed. This genocide became known as the Holocaust.

CHAPTER 1

Buchenwald survivors cooking

It was nice to feel free—the first time I felt free for many years. Freedom is the most precious commodity! ... But to be free was a circumstance that was completely strange. To be able to wake up and know you could go outside the perimeter of wherever you were and nobody would challenge, "Where are you going?" It's the most wonderful feeling of all—freedom!

—*Harry Lowi, who as a Czech Jewish youth escaped from a concentration camp near Ebensee*

LIBERATION

In the spring of 1945, near the end of World War II in Europe, Adolf Hitler's German army in Berlin was pinned on three sides by Soviet troops. U.S. soldiers approached from the west, marching to victory across the German countryside. But these tough, battle-tested infantrymen weren't prepared for what they discovered beyond the tall gates and barbed-wire fences of the prison camps at Buchenwald and Dachau.

At first these concentration camps appeared to be places where people were forced to work in support of the German war effort. Upon closer inspection, a much more sinister truth began to emerge. These were death camps where tens of thousands of people had been tortured, shot, or gassed. Then many were cremated to conceal the awful truth. In some camps prisoners were forced to work themselves to death in fields or factories, or to break up rocks in quarries until they died of disease or starvation. Even those who

Survivors looked on as U.S. soldiers and members of the press inspected the barracks at Dachau.

managed to survive the cold, diseases, and brutality of the camps looked like living skeletons.

Entering a Nazi concentration camp, American soldier Leon Bass was shaken by what he observed. "I saw human beings who had been beaten, starved and tortured," he said. "They were standing there skin and bones, dressed in striped pajamas. They had skeletal faces with deep set eyes. They had sores on their bodies. One man held out his hands. And they were webbed together with scabs, due to malnutrition."

As the war was ending, an Allied victory was at hand. The Nazis were in full retreat, and Allied troops marched from camp to camp, freeing survivors. But the death and desperation they saw shook them to the core. In some camps corpses were stacked like firewood. Other bodies were heaped in piles, because people were dying faster than their bodies could be burned or buried. Many survivors were so thin that their bones protruded from their skin. Survivors streamed to greet the soldiers, some crawling on their hands and knees to get a glimpse of their rescuers. Some greeted them with cheers. Others reached out to touch them, to see whether they were truly real. Some were too weak and confused to react at all.

"Timidly, we looked around and glanced at each other questioningly," wrote Viktor Frankl, a Viennese doctor who was a prisoner at the Türkheim camp in Germany. "Then we ventured a few steps out of the camp. This time no orders were shouted at us, nor was there any need to duck quickly to avoid a blow or a kick.

"'Freedom'—we repeated to ourselves, and yet we could not grasp it."

Telling the World

Until Allied soldiers saw the camps, few of them could grasp the scope of the Nazis' Final Solution. They had read news reports of the camps, but some suspected they were exaggerated. When U.S. generals Dwight D. Eisenhower and George S. Patton saw the camps, they quickly realized that the situation was far worse than had been reported.

"I have never felt able to describe my emotional reactions when I first came face to face with indisputable evidence of Nazi brutality and ruthless disregard of every shred of decency," Eisenhower wrote. "I visited every nook and cranny of the camp because I felt it my duty to be in a position from then on to testify at first hand about these things in case there ever grew up at home the belief or assumption that the 'stories of Nazi brutality were just propaganda.'"

Some Allied soldiers were so disgusted by what they had discovered that they rounded up nearby townspeople and brought them to see the camps for themselves. They did not want German

Generals Dwight Eisenhower, George Patton, and Omar Bradley and other U.S. Army officers viewed the bodies of prisoners killed before the liberation of the Nazi concentration camp at Ohrdruf, Germany.

citizens to be able to say they never saw what had occurred in the camps. Eisenhower invited the press corps to film, photograph, and write about the horrors of the concentration camps. The world would need to see proof of what had happened. Otherwise people might never believe it.

Survivor Stories

The arrival of Allied soldiers made survivors who had the energy jump and scream for joy. They were saved, and they were shocked.

Citizens of Ludwigslust, Germany, were ordered to visit a nearby concentration camp.

As time passed, however, their jubilation turned to a mix of relief, sorrow, and confusion. While concentration camp prisoners were grateful to be rescued, many struggled after their release. They were alone and did not know whether their family members had survived. Most had not. Many survivors were ill or injured, and most were unsure what to do next.

"We had lost our families, our homes," wrote Hadassah Bimko, who was freed from the Bergen-Belsen camp. "We had no place to go, nobody to hug, nobody who was waiting for us, anywhere. We had been liberated from death and from the fear of death, but we were not free from the fear of life."

The Allies quickly set up displaced-persons camps for survivors. Few of the survivors had homes to return to, so many remained at the concentration camps where they had been imprisoned. They were liberated, but they were still, in a sense, not free. Those who returned to their homelands often faced taunts and discrimination from non-Jews. Victor Breitburg, who survived the war in the Lodz

Newspapermen talked with survivors at a hospital in the newly liberated Buchenwald concentration camp.

ghetto, had that experience when he went home to Krakow, Poland.

"I arrived in Krakow around noon," he said. "I saw a man who was still wearing the stripes from the concentration camp. As I tried to approach him, two Polish people started to question him. 'Hey, Jew, where are you going? Why aren't you going to Palestine? We don't want you here!' I was dumbfounded. I saw tears come down the man's face, and nobody came to his defense. I was scared too, and angry. How dare they? ... I felt that the multitude of people was looking at me. I met their glare of hate with my own hate. I felt like shouting at them: 'You didn't help us; you turned us in; you are worse than the Germans.'"

Sometimes the situation was even worse than taunting. Forty-two concentration camp survivors were killed July 4, 1946, by an anti-Jewish mob in Kielce, Poland.

I rode on coal trains, stopped army trucks. It took me six days to make the 600 miles to Diepholz. As I walked from the main road to the [displaced-persons] camp, I saw far away two young women on the road, walking in my direction. My heart started to pound, and sure enough, there was my wife! Can you imagine our meeting?

—Jules Zaidenweber, Jewish survivor of a concentration camp near Vaihingen, Germany

Jewish family in a displaced-persons camp, 1948

CHAPTER 2

REMEMBERING, REBUILDING, AND RELOCATING

For many survivors, freedom did not end their nightmare. They had lost their entire families. Their homes were destroyed. They had no jobs and no money. Many were troubled by guilt, asking themselves "Why me? Why did I survive?"

As they began rebuilding their lives, many survivors, having been so close to death, came to realize what was truly important in life. They were committed to their community, to their faith, to love, and to starting new families. Many women who had lost their husbands during the war married men who had lost their wives.

"I am alone. I have no one. I have lost everything," a survivor said in a marriage proposal to his new love. "You are alone. You have no one. You have lost everything. Let us be alone together."

Rabbis had to revise Jewish law on remarriage. Traditionally a widow was allowed to remarry only if there were witnesses to her husband's death. That evidence was almost impossible to get after the

Portrait of wedding celebrants in a displaced-persons camp in Kassel, Germany

Holocaust. So rabbis soon began to allow remarriage for those whose spouses had been sent to death camps or were presumed dead.

As new couples wed, new families formed. One Jewish community put up posters proudly reporting an increase in birthrates. Many Jewish couples deliberately had a lot of children, eager to increase the population of Jews that had been decimated during the war.

A Legacy of Large Families

Yitta Schwartz and her family survived the Bergen-Belsen concentration camp and moved to the United States in 1953 to start their lives over. When they arrived in the primarily Jewish community of Williamsburg, in Brooklyn, New York, the Schwartz family already had 11 children. Eventually they had five more.

When Yitta died, in January 2010, she was 93 years old. Her 15 surviving children had given her more than 200 grandchildren and so many great- and great-great-grandchildren that her family estimated she had more than 2,000 direct descendants. Yitta's family became one of the largest clans ever produced by a Holocaust survivor. Though she considered bearing children a tribute to God, Yitta's devotion to a large family was also a rejection of Hitler's Final Solution.

Reluctant to let her picture be taken, Yitta often said: "Just keep me in your heart. If you leave a child or grandchild, you live forever."

Piecing Together the Past

Fearing that the past would be forgotten, some of those whose families and communities had been destroyed during the war created memorial books called *yizkor* books. The books recorded the history of towns' residents, religious leaders, and social institutions that had been wiped out by the Holocaust and the Nazis. In some cases yizkor books are among the few remaining records showing that such people, places, and organizations ever existed.

While all yizkor books are different, most have similar features.

A photo in a yizkor book for the town of Sosnowiec, Poland, with an arrow pointing to Gila Grynwald, who died in Auschwitz when she was 21

The text is in Hebrew or Yiddish. Most books include town histories, descriptions of daily life, and accounts of the Holocaust's impact on the towns. A list of Holocaust victims is usually included, and details about postwar life. In the Yizkor Book of Gombin, Poland, survivor Jack Frankel recalled his experiences at a concentration camp.

"Arriving in camp, we were greeted by a spectacle prepared by the Nazis for the new inhabitants," he wrote. "In the middle of an open area the Nazis had built four gallows, placing a Jewish boy of ten or eleven near each one. The Nazis informed all assembled that the four criminals had been caught smuggling food. A crime for which they were about to pay with their lives. The noose was then placed around the little neck of each child. German justice was then carried out (four helpless Jewish children swinging on the gallows)."

Anguish into Art

Survivors of the Holocaust coped with their experiences in various ways. For some, talking about what they had lived through was too painful. Others found comfort in writing about the experience. Some wanted to help people understand what they had endured and to make a historic record of the events. They wrote letters, memoirs, poems, and books. Some turned their grief into art by painting, sculpting, or making music.

Even before the Holocaust, many artists had been committed to recording what they had endured. They had seen Nazi storm troopers raid libraries, art museums, and galleries and steal artwork and burn books they thought were anti-German. The Nazis removed any works they believed promoted undesirable ideas or lifestyles.

During the war Jewish artists couldn't work as freely as they had in the past. But many were determined to continue despite the risks. One such artist was Charlotte Buresova. Her sketches of mothers and their children showed the hope that existed among Jewish people despite the terrible conditions of the war and the Holocaust. "[I was determined to] oppose the disaster with beauty and sketch all the incredible things I saw," she said.

In concentration camps artists secretly sketched on bathroom walls, in their bunkhouses, and in other places where Nazi guards wouldn't see them. Some of

Charlotte Buresova's portrait of Jirina Kanova, who died in Auschwitz

their art showed the horrible conditions in the camps, and they knew that if they were caught, the punishment would likely be death. After the war many pieces of concentration camp art were all that remained of the artists and what they had endured.

Writers Elie Wiesel and Anne Frank

Among writers who survived the Holocaust, perhaps none became more famous and influential than Elie Wiesel. His book *Night* recounts his experiences as a 15-year-old prisoner at the Auschwitz and Buchenwald camps.

When Wiesel's family arrived at Auschwitz, the men and women

After surviving the Holocaust, Elie Wiesel studied in Paris, France, and became a journalist and author.

were immediately separated. Elie and his father went left; his mother and sisters went right. Not until years later did he discover that his mother and one of his sisters were taken straight to the gas chamber.

"For a part of a second I glimpsed my mother and my sisters moving away to the right," he wrote. "Tzipora held Mother's hand. I saw them disappear into the distance; my mother was stroking my sister's fair hair ... and I did not know that in that place, at that moment, I was parting from my mother and Tzipora forever."

Among those who did not survive, Anne Frank remains one of the most important writers of the Holocaust era. As a 13-year-old

Anne Frank's famous diary charts her life from 1942 to 1944.

girl whose family hid in a secret annex in Nazi-occupied Amsterdam, Anne documented the details of her days and wrote of her hopes, fears, and dreams. Her writings, each addressed to her diary, which she called Kitty, were filled with the fears, desires, and other thoughts of a normal teenager. But they also reflected wisdom that is uncommon in someone her age. Hearing a radio report that American and British armies were invading France to liberate Europe from the Nazis, Anne wrote on June 6, 1944:

> *Oh, Kitty, the best part of the invasion is that I have the feeling that friends are approaching. We have been oppressed by those terrible Germans for so long, they have had their knives so at our throats, that the thought of friends and delivery fills us with confidence! Now it doesn't concern the Jews anymore; no, it concerns Holland and all occupied Europe. Perhaps, Margot says, I might be able to go back to school in September or October.*

Just two months later, Nazi police discovered the Frank family's hiding place. Anne was sent first to Auschwitz, then to the Bergen-Belsen concentration camp in Germany. In February or March 1945, she died of typhus. She was just 15 years old. Her father, Otto Frank, survived the Holocaust. He had Anne's diary published, and soon it inspired plays and movies.

Artists Marc Chagall and David Olère

After barely escaping Nazi clutches, Marc Chagall went on to become one of the most successful artists of the 20th century. Chagall was a Jew born in Russia who lived most of his life in France. German critics had praised his paintings, but the Nazis called his artwork degenerate and seized it. Chagall and his family barely survived the Holocaust by staying a step ahead of the soldiers who were rounding up and killing Jews throughout Europe. His family fled France and moved to the United States in 1941 to evade the Nazis.

Chagall returned to France in 1948. He saw that the war had left Jewish communities in tatters and much of Europe in ruins. From that point on, his artwork reflected the sadness he felt about what he saw.

Marc Chagall was a world-famous painter and stained-glass artist.

For a book about Jewish artists killed under Nazi rule, Chagall wrote a poem that later inspired his painting *Song of David*:

> I see the fire, the smoke and the gas; rising to the blue cloud, turning it black. I see the torn-out hair, the pulled-out teeth. They overwhelm me with my rabid palette. I stand in the desert before heaps of boots, clothing, ash and dung, and mumble my Kaddish [Jewish prayer for the dead]. And as I stand—from my paintings, the painted David descends to me, harp in hand. He wants to help me weep and recite chapters of Psalms.

When Nazis at Auschwitz discovered that David Olère was a talented artist and knew several languages, they spared him from the gas chamber. They gave him bits of bread and ordered him to create colorful postcards and letters for their wives and children. He also had the grim task of clearing the dead from gas chambers and the crematorium.

After he was freed, Olère drew what he had seen. His art includes images of wide-eyed, horrified figures, often tattooed with his own inmate number. His pictures of the gas chambers and killing methods are important because there are no photographs of these operations.

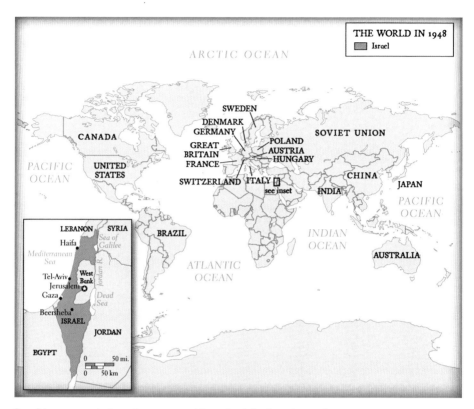

THE WORLD IN 1948
■ Israel

ARCTIC OCEAN

SWEDEN
DENMARK
GERMANY
CANADA
GREAT
BRITAIN
FRANCE
POLAND
AUSTRIA
HUNGARY
SOVIET UNION

PACIFIC
OCEAN
UNITED
STATES
SWITZERLAND ITALY □
see inset
CHINA
INDIA
JAPAN

PACIFIC
OCEAN

LEBANON   SYRIA
Haifa
Mediterranean
Sea
Sea of
Galilee
Tel-Aviv
Jerusalem
Gaza
West
Bank
Beersheba
ISRAEL
Dead
Sea
JORDAN
EGYPT
0   50 mi.
0   50 km
BRAZIL
ATLANTIC
OCEAN
INDIAN
OCEAN
AUSTRALIA

Israel became an independent state and homeland for Jews in 1948.

The Birth of Israel

Perhaps the most lasting and important legacy of the Holocaust is

the birth of Israel. After the Holocaust few Jews knew where to go

next. For centuries Jewish people had lacked a home country. But

on May 14, 1948, the country of Israel, on the eastern shore of the

Mediterranean Sea, declared its independence from Great Britain.

Israel would be the Jews' homeland.

Jews who had been uprooted during the Holocaust began

streaming to Israel in search of refuge and new lives. Jews who felt threatened in Arab countries also made their way to Israel. From 1948 to 1958, the population of Israel soared from 800,000 to 2 million, most of them Jewish. In 1949 Peter Somogyi was one of the Jews to find refuge in Israel. He had survived horrendous experiments at the hands of Nazi doctors during World War II. Somogyi fled Hungary and made his way to southern Italy to catch a ship to his new homeland.

"We waited for the boat that was to take us to Israel," he said. "There were hundreds of us by then, gathered from every corner of

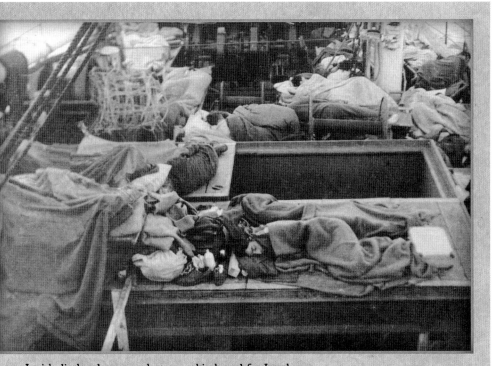

Jewish displaced persons slept on a ship bound for Israel.

Europe, awaiting passage to the Promised Land. We were all very excited. We felt for the first time that we didn't have to look behind our back and hear someone saying, 'dirty Jew.'"

The creation of Israel, the result of dividing Palestine into a Jewish state and an Arab state, gave millions of Jews a place to call home, but maintaining that home has not been easy. Many Arabs in neighboring countries—and even within Israel—insist the land is rightfully theirs. Some of the disputes between Arabs and Jews have resulted in bloody clashes and wars.

In the United States after World War II, racial segregation—the separation of blacks and whites in schools and other public places—was still widely practiced throughout the South in former slave states. Racism and discrimination were also common in other parts of the country. In the U.S. armed forces, units of black soldiers and airmen were separated from white units. The Holocaust revealed how such practices could put a country on the path to something more sinister.

Nations around the world began adopting new laws to guard against racism so nothing like the Holocaust could ever happen again. Germany's constitution, adopted in 1949, forbade discrimination based on race. The U.S. civil rights movement made major strides against racism in the 1950s and 1960s. In 1964 U.S. President Lyndon

Civil rights march from Selma to Montgomery, Alabama, in 1965

Johnson signed the Civil Rights Act. It banned discrimination based on race, sex, religion, or national origin in employment practices and public facilities. In the 1980s and 1990s in South Africa, the practice of apartheid, which had kept black and white South Africans bitterly divided, began to erode. In 1994 the country elected Nelson Mandela president in its first multiracial and democratic elections.

Generals Dwight Eisenhower (right), Omar Bradley (left), and George Patton inspected stolen art hidden in a salt mine in Merkers, Germany.

THE PURSUIT OF JUSTICE

After World War II ended and concentration camp survivors had been freed, the world called for justice. A series of war crimes trials by courts known as military tribunals were held at the Palace of Justice in Nuremberg, Germany. Leading the proceedings were judges and prosecutors from the victorious Allied forces—the United States, Britain, France, and the Soviet Union.

Even before the end of the war, Allied leaders had been discussing how to

There is one group to which the method of annihilation was applied on a scale so immense that it is my duty to refer separately to the evidence. I mean the extermination of the Jews. If there were no other crime against the men, this alone, in which all of them were implicated, would suffice. History holds no parallel to these horrors.

—*Sir Hartley Shawcross, chief British prosecutor, 1946*
Nuremberg trials of the Nazis

punish the Nazis after they were defeated. Although the Allied leaders considered executing as many as 50,000 Nazi officials without trials, they finally decided that justice could only be served if they followed due process.

But they would never be able to bring Hitler to justice. With Berlin in ruins and his soldiers in full retreat, Hitler realized he could never win the war. Yet he refused to surrender. Hiding in a bunker beneath the German Chancellery, Hitler killed himself on April 30, 1945. But prosecutors pursued former Nazi officers, soldiers, guards, judges, public officials, and business owners who directly participated in the genocide or helped in the effort. Many of the highest-ranking Nazi leaders and worst offenders were brought to trial from October 1945 to October 1946.

Some Nazis who knew they were going to be caught, convicted, and perhaps even executed, fled overseas after the war to escape punishment. Some killed themselves before they could be captured. Along with his wife, Joseph Goebbels, Hitler's minister of propaganda, poisoned their six young children. Then Goebbels likely shot his wife and then himself shortly before Germany's surrender. Heinrich Himmler, one of the most powerful leaders in Germany, had ordered the killing of millions of people during the war. He killed himself by biting on a poison capsule when he was captured. Some who were brought to trial were defiant and unwilling to let justice be carried out. One defendant, Robert Ley, a Nazi politician and close adviser to

Joseph Goebbels with his wife, Magda, their six children, and Magda's son, Harald Quandt, from her first marriage; Harald (in uniform) was the only child to survive the war

Hitler, killed himself during the trials. Hermann Goering, considered one of Hitler's closest and most powerful advisers, took poison in his cell the night before his scheduled execution.

But 21 of the most notorious Nazi leaders and Holocaust creators remained to face trial at Nuremberg. The charges included crimes against peace, conspiracy to commit crimes against peace, war crimes, and crimes against humanity. Crimes against humanity included such Holocaust-related actions as murder, enslavement, deportation of a civilian population, and persecution on political, racial, or religious grounds.

Represented by German defense lawyers, the Nazis repeatedly gave the same excuse. They said they were just following orders. Many claimed they were not responsible. They blamed somebody further up the chain of command. They said they had sworn an oath of loyalty to Hitler and would have been killed had they not upheld it. Nuremberg's judges were not persuaded by those arguments.

U.S. Supreme Court Justice Robert Jackson led the prosecution team from the United States. In his opening statement, he said, "In the prisoners' dock sit twenty-odd broken men. ... Merely as individuals, their fate is of little consequence in the world.

"What makes this inquest significant is that these prisoners ... are the living symbols of racial hatreds, of terrorism and violence, and of the arrogance and cruelty of power. ... Civilization can afford no compromise with the social forces which would gain renewed strength if we deal ambiguously or indecisively with the men in whom these forces now precariously survive."

Jackson and the other judges saw the Nuremberg trials as an opportunity to send a message to the world that such actions would never again be tolerated. Of the 21 defendants, 14 were sentenced to death. The others received varying prison sentences depending on whether they had been directly involved in ordering the killings or had let them happen.

After the first military tribunals, more trials were held in Nuremberg and several other cities in occupied Germany. In those trials 185 defendants faced prosecution for their involvement in the Holocaust. Doctors were tried for murder and for conducting horrific experiments on prisoners.

Robert Jackson was the lead prosecutor for the United States during the Nuremberg trials.

The defendants (center two rows), under heavy guard, during the Nuremberg trials

Officers who had been in mobile killing squads were tried for the slaughter of civilians. Commanders of concentration camps and guards were tried for the murders that occurred in them. Judges were tried for allowing Germany's legal system to tolerate mass murder. Executives of I.G. Farben, the company that made Zyklon B, a poison gas used to kill millions, were put on trial with the heads of other German war industries.

Most of the U.S. trials resulted in convictions. But soon after the trials ended, parole boards were created and clemency was granted to many of those who had behaved well in prison. Many who had been sentenced to death were spared. Few of those directly responsible for the Holocaust were ultimately punished for their actions.

Yet the Nuremberg trials have had a lasting impact. The trials set new standards for international law. They created clear rules about the treatment of enemies and citizens in times of both peace and war.

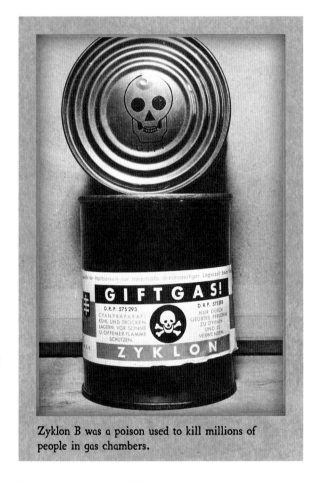

Zyklon B was a poison used to kill millions of people in gas chambers.

The methods used at Nuremberg also became the model for trials used in modern-day instances of genocide, including mass killings in the Balkans and Rwanda during the 1990s.

Nazi Hunters

Knowing they were going to be tried and probably convicted, many of the Nazis responsible for the Holocaust fled to other countries. Rome, Italy, became a popular hideout. Some Roman Catholic priests and public officials there offered sanctuary to such notable Nazis as Adolf Eichmann, one of the main architects of the Holocaust, and Walter Rauff and Otto Wachter, both high-ranking officers who directed Hitler's storm troopers.

Countries in South America, particularly Argentina, were also common places for Nazi war criminals to hide. The United States became home for some Nazis who pretended to be anti-Communists seeking refuge from the Soviet Union. Many of the fugitives changed their names and appearances. They tried to cover up their pasts in order to start their lives over.

Simon Wiesenthal wasn't going to let them off so easily. After surviving the Holocaust, Wiesenthal became a Nazi hunter soon after his liberation from the Mauthausen camp in Austria in May 1945. Within two years Wiesenthal opened a center in his hometown of Linz, Austria, where he collected evidence to find former Nazis and bring the war criminals to trial. While the effort couldn't bring back Holocaust victims, it was a comfort to some survivors to see justice being done. Wiesenthal made it his life's work.

"Survival is a privilege which entails obligations," Wiesenthal wrote. "I am forever asking myself what I can do for those who have not survived. The answer I have found for myself (and which need not necessarily be the answer for every survivor) is: I want to be their

Simon Wiesenthal was a Holocaust survivor who spent the rest of his life tracking down Nazi war criminals and fighting anti-Semitism and prejudice against all people.

mouthpiece, I want to keep their memory alive, to make sure the dead live on in that memory."

Other famous Nazi hunters included Tuvia Friedman, Serge and Beate Klarsfeld, Michel Thomas, Elliot Welles, and Efraim Zuroff.

Israel itself became perhaps the most famous Nazi hunter in 1960 when it landed one of the biggest postwar catches of a Holocaust criminal. Acting on tips that Adolf Eichmann was living and working in Buenos Aires, Argentina, a group of Israeli secret service agents captured him and brought him to Israel for trial. Eichmann, long regarded as one of the masterminds behind the Holocaust, was convicted and hanged.

Seeking Payback

Not only did the Holocaust result in the murder of 6 million Jewish men, women, and children, it also included the greatest theft in history. Nazis stole anything they could from Jewish families across Europe. They raided Jewish museums, synagogues, and private homes. They stole art, jewelry, and anything else of value. Some have estimated that Hitler's henchmen stole property worth $230 billion to $320 billion in today's dollars.

Since the 1950s Germany has paid $70 billion to an agency representing Jewish victims of the Holocaust. But that is a fraction

Defendant Adolf Eichmann (left, in the booth) listened in court as he was sentenced to death.

of the money owed. Many survivors of the Holocaust and victims' families still have not been fully compensated for their losses.

The effort gained new momentum in 1996 when three lawsuits were filed in New York on behalf of Holocaust survivors and their heirs. One of the early targets of the lawsuits were several large Swiss banks. Before and during World War II, thousands of Jewish families deposited their life savings in Swiss banks. The families hoped the banks' strict privacy rules would protect their money from the Nazis.

Burt Neuborne, lead attorney for the Holocaust survivors' lawsuit against Swiss banks

When the war ended, survivors went to Switzerland to claim their families' money, but they were turned away. They were told they needed a death certificate to get the money—something the Nazis did not issue during their mass exterminations.

European insurance companies were also sued in American courts for failing to pay on life insurance policies and annuities many Jews had bought before the war. The policies and annuities were meant to provide some financial security for remaining family members if some of them died prematurely. When it came time to pay, many of the German, Swiss, French, and Italian insurance firms refused. They also claimed they needed proof of a family member's death.

The third set of lawsuits involves the theft of valuable Jewish possessions, including art collections that were stolen in Europe and resold in the United States. By some estimates, Nazis looted 20 percent of the most valuable art in Europe, from Jews and non-Jews alike. American museums hold art that was stolen by the Nazis. As part of the museums' accreditation processes, they must show that they are trying to identify the owners of works the museums bought during the Nazi years. Finally, through the American justice system, families of the original Jewish owners have a chance to reclaim their lost art.

So far the victims groups have had mixed results in court. The Swiss banks settled the lawsuits against them in August 1998 by agreeing to pay $1.25 billion to families of Jewish account holders. In 2004 a U.S. federal judge dismissed one set of Holocaust insurance claims cases on the ground that the disputes should instead be settled by a special commission. Efforts by some families to reclaim art taken by the Nazis often take years to show results. Identifying the original ownership and possession of such priceless works requires case-by-case examination, which is a long process.

A work of art stolen by Nazis was returned to the family of the rightful owner as part of a settlement in a New York lawsuit.

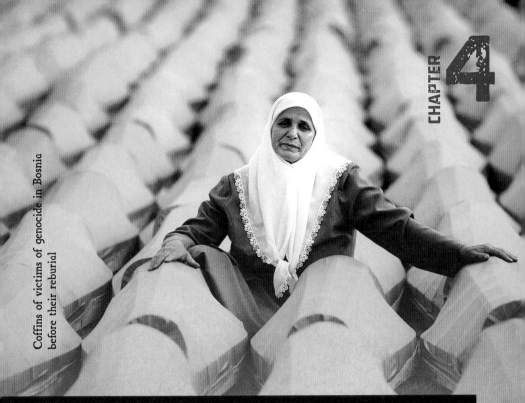

CHAPTER 4

Coffins of victims of genocide in Bosnia before their reburial

I think that every person on earth should examine this, what has happened in the Holocaust, because a thing like that can happen again and we need to watch that it should never happen again to any minority. And therefore I feel I need to get this across to the world, maybe even to our future generation, and tell them that this cruelty has been done to people from other people and to watch out.

—Helen Lebowitz Goldkind, who as a teenager survived Auschwitz

GUARDING AGAINST GENOCIDE

After the Holocaust the world struggled to answer the question "How could this have happened?" Many were already asking, "How can we keep it from happening again?" World leaders gathered at the United Nations December 9, 1948, three years after the end of World War II. The U.N. quickly adopted the Convention on the Prevention and Punishment of the Crime of Genocide. It was intended as a response to the claims of the Nuremberg defendants that they had broken no laws. It also made clear that the attempted mass murder of an entire people—whether during wartime or not—would not be tolerated.

Ethnic Cleansing and Modern Genocides

One question that has lingered since the Holocaust is whether something so terrible could happen again. Many people have argued that it already has happened and that, in some places, it continues today.

In the 1970s more than 1 million Cambodians died because of forced labor, disease, torture, starvation, and execution under the brutal rule of dictator Pol Pot and his Khmer Rouge government. Most were killed because of their political beliefs, their education, or their religious backgrounds.

From 1992 to 1995, military units and some civilian Serbian forces in the country formerly called Yugoslavia mounted a horrific campaign against Bosnian Muslims. Serbs intent on creating an ethnically pure new republic of Bosnia and Herzegovina worried that letting Bosnian Muslims remain would thwart their efforts. So Serbians began forcibly relocating the Muslims to non-Serb areas or killing them. Serbian soldiers and militia members tore men and boys from their homes and shot them before abusing their mothers and sisters. Some called the action an act of war or an ethnic

Tourists looked at photos of victims of the Khmer Rouge at the Tuol Sleng Genocide Museum in Cambodia's capital, Phnom Penh.

cleansing campaign. Others declared it genocide. In the end, as many as 200,000 men and boys had been murdered in the worst mass killings in Europe since World War II. More than 2 million Bosnians were forced from their homes as part of the aggression. Some of those responsible were brought to trial, where a judge determined that their actions amounted to genocide.

"They targeted for extinction the 40,000 Bosnian Muslims living in Srebrenica, a group which was emblematic of the Bosnian Muslims in general," the judge said. "They stripped all the male

Muslim prisoners, military and civilian, elderly and young, of their personal belongings and identification, and deliberately and methodically killed them solely on the basis of their identity."

In the small African country of Rwanda in 1994, more than 800,000 people were killed for being members of the Tutsi ethnic group or for being moderate Hutu. The killing spree, carried out by members of the Hutu Power extremist group, lasted just 100 days, but it left more than 20 percent of Rwanda's population dead. The Hutu extremists accused the Tutsis of accumulating too much power, and they spread lies claiming that Tutsis were going to try to oppress and enslave Hutus.

When Rwanda's Hutu president died in a suspicious plane crash, Hutu extremists blamed all Tutsis. They killed any Tutsis they could find and ordered Hutus to kill their Tutsi neighbors or risk being killed themselves. Today, while Rwanda still struggles with ethnic tensions, the mass killings have ended, and the country has established a more organized form of government with open elections.

Even now many consider the continuing ethnic conflict in the Darfur region of Sudan as genocide and are urging international forces to stop the killings. After decades of oppression, African tribes formed armed rebel groups that in 2003 began fighting back against government-supported Arab militias. The president of Sudan has

Jewish World Watch sponsored a Walk for Darfur to raise awareness and support for the survivors of genocide.

been indicted for genocide by the International Criminal Court in The Hague, in the Netherlands.

Continued Anti-Semitism and Racial Hatred

As much progress as the world has made since the Holocaust, anti-Semitism—a hatred of, or prejudice against, Jewish people—still remains. Synagogues are still targets of anti-Semitic graffiti. The Internet has become a haven for hate speech and bigotry. Websites filled with racial, ethnic, and religious slurs promote negative stereotypes or even encourage violence against certain groups.

Swastikas were painted on headstones at a Jewish cemetery in St. Petersburg, Russia. More than 50 of the graves were vandalized in February 2004.

News sites that invite readers to comment on racially charged stories often receive torrents of racist rantings, threats, and bullying.

Some groups work to stop such activity. Formed in 1913 in a small Chicago office long before the Holocaust, the Anti-Defamation League (ADL) was created to respond to speech, writing, and other activities that are hateful or harmful to Jews. Today the ADL's role is to fight anti-Semitism and other forms of bigotry, to defend democratic ideals, and to protect the civil rights of everyone.

Since 1987 the ADL has given the Courage to Care award to

people who worked to rescue Jews during the Holocaust without asking for anything in return. Recipients are given plaques that honor heroism during the Holocaust.

Human Rights Organizations

The U.N. General Assembly adopted a Universal Declaration of Human Rights in 1948. The nonbinding declaration was a response to the horrors of the Holocaust and other incidents during World

The United Nations, meeting in Paris in 1948, adopted the Universal Declaration of Human Rights.

War II. The declaration urges member nations to promote basic human rights as the "foundation of freedom, justice and peace in the world."

Today several international organizations work to prevent violations of human rights. One is Amnesty International, which was founded in 1961. Amnesty International is a nonprofit organization that works to prevent human rights abuses around the world. With 2.8 million members in more than 150 countries, the organization is one of the most prominent human rights groups in the world. Another group, Human Rights Watch, was established in 1978 to monitor activities of Soviet leaders. Today it tracks human rights abuses and violations throughout the world, defends victims, and seeks to punish offenders.

The U.N. in 2006 established the Human Rights Council to replace the United Nations Commission on Human Rights, which had been active since 1946. The Human Rights Council was set up "to weave the international legal fabric that protects our fundamental rights and freedoms." The council's role has expanded over time to allow it to respond to a variety of human rights problems. It also serves as a forum where human rights defenders can voice their concerns.

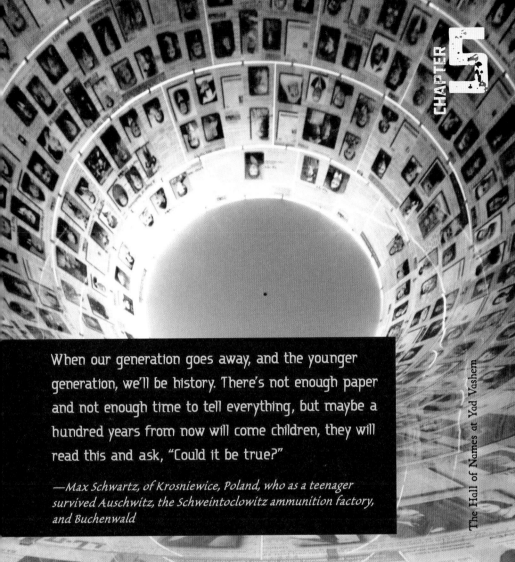

CHAPTER 5

> When our generation goes away, and the younger generation, we'll be history. There's not enough paper and not enough time to tell everything, but maybe a hundred years from now will come children, they will read this and ask, "Could it be true?"
>
> —*Max Schwartz, of Krosniewice, Poland, who as a teenager survived Auschwitz, the Schweintoclowitz ammunition factory, and Buchenwald*

The Hall of Names at Yad Vashem

HOLOCAUST REMEMBRANCE AND HONOR

With each passing year, there are fewer and fewer Holocaust survivors and fewer still who can fully recount the horrors they endured. Keeping those memories alive, honoring those who died, and preventing a repeat of such atrocities are the main purpose of the museums, monuments, memorials, scholarships, awards, and other remembrances created since the Holocaust.

Museums, Monuments, and Memorials

After the war and the liberation of concentration camp survivors, memorials and other tributes to Holocaust victims and survivors began appearing across Europe. Those who had endured the nightmare of the Holocaust, and others who had witnessed it, were determined not to let the world forget what had happened.

Established in 1953, Israel's Yad Vashem has the largest Holocaust document collection in the world. It also is home to the largest Holocaust-related artifact collection. Its Hall of Remembrance contains an eternal flame as a tribute to Holocaust

Yad Vashem, in Jerusalem, Israel, welcomes about 800,000 visitors a year.

victims, as well as the names of 22 of the concentration camps where they died. The Hall of Names contains 600 photographs of Holocaust victims.

Since the United States Holocaust Memorial Museum opened in Washington, D.C., in 1993, about 30 million visitors have passed by these words engraved on the wall in the museum's Hall of Witness: "You are my witnesses." The museum encourages visitors to speak out and act against anti-Semitism, ethnic violence, genocide, and other crimes against humanity.

Filled with personal belongings, photographs, writings, and other mementos of Holocaust victims and survivors, the Holocaust Memorial Museum leaves a powerful impression. Visitors can tour a railcar that carried prisoners to concentration camps. An exhibit with hundreds of shoes taken from Holocaust victims is especially moving. A model of the gas chambers and crematoriums at Auschwitz illustrates the scope and chilling efficiency of the Nazis' killing operation.

There are other Holocaust museums in the United States, including ones in California, Florida, Illinois, Michigan, New York, Texas, and Virginia. There are also Holocaust museums in Argentina, Australia, Belgium, Canada, England, France, Germany, Italy, and Japan. Some of the European concentration camp sites

Visitors at the Tower of Faces at the United States Holocaust
Memorial Museum in Washington, D.C.

also have become museums and provide public tours of the grounds and memorials to victims.

Germany and Germans

As those who elected Hitler, gave him his power, served in his armies, and carried out so much of the horror of the Holocaust, Germans have had to spend much of the time since the war making amends for their actions—or their inaction in allowing the Holocaust to happen. After World War II, West Germany banned all relics of its Nazi past. Nazi flags, emblems, literature, and brown uniforms were all prohibited. It also became a crime to encourage hate against a religion, ethnic group, or nationality. In 1985 it became a crime to deny that the Holocaust happened. West Germany also placed restrictions on its own army, including blocking it from acting beyond the country's borders. Starting in 1953 West Germany began paying reparations to Holocaust victims for their injuries, health problems, and time spent in prison camps.

After the war it was hard for Germans to discuss the Holocaust and their roles in it. Many refused to admit what they had or had not done—whether they had supported Hitler, turned in Jews, or worked as soldiers. Most Germans claimed they had not known that Jewish people were being systematically killed. But they all knew Jews

German schoolboys lined up to return their Nazi-oriented textbooks to their principal in Berlin in August 1945.

had been treated unfairly—that they could be fired from their jobs, kicked out of school, and arrested or beat up for being Jewish. Still the truth proved too painful for many Germans to confront. Instead they decided to ignore anything related to the Nazis and focused on rebuilding their lives and their country, much of which had been destroyed in the war.

It wasn't until the U.S. TV miniseries *Holocaust* was broadcast in West Germany in 1979 that many Germans were willing to talk about their nation's dark past. About half the country's adult population watched at least one of the episodes. Suddenly the Holocaust was being discussed in German classrooms and debated by German writers, historians, and politicians. West Germany canceled the time limit for prosecuting people accused of Nazi war crimes. Since 1996 Germans have paid tribute to Holocaust

The Holocaust on Film

Hollywood has tried to honor the memory of the Holocaust. The first major Holocaust film to attract a wide audience was 1959's *The Diary of Anne Frank*. Based on the young girl's diary, the film details the Frank family's frightening years spent hiding in the annex of an office building in Nazi-occupied Amsterdam. The film generated an interest in the Holocaust among Germans who were too young to remember the horrors of the war.

Among the most notable and successful attempts to portray the Holocaust was the movie *Schindler's List*. Directed by Steven Spielberg, the 1993 film tells the true story of Oskar Schindler, a German factory owner who worked to save more than 1,200 of his Jewish employees from being hauled off to Nazi concentration camps.

The 1997 film *Life Is Beautiful* features a Jewish man using his cunning wit to win the love of a beautiful woman. He later uses the same cunning wit to protect his young son from the horrors of a Nazi concentration camp. The 2002 film *The Pianist* tells the true story of a young musician who survived the Holocaust in the ruins of the Warsaw ghetto. The 2008 movie *The Boy in the Striped Pajamas* tells the tale of a Nazi commandant's 8-year-old son's forbidden friendship with a prisoner his age.

The Holocaust Memorial in Berlin, Germany, includes 2,711 concrete slabs, one for each page of the Talmud, a Jewish holy book.

victims on January 27, the anniversary of the liberation of Auschwitz. A large Holocaust memorial was dedicated in the center of Berlin, Germany's capital, in 2005. It is a field of 2,711 concrete slabs arranged in a waving grid over 5 acres (2 hectares) near the Brandenburg Gate.

Looking Back and Looking Ahead

The final tally of Hitler's Final Solution is staggering. From 1933 to 1945, about two-thirds of Europe's Jews were murdered. In some cities the entire Jewish population was wiped out. Millions of people were killed simply for being who they were.

While the human toll of the Holocaust was huge and left lasting scars on many survivors and their families, over the years positive legacies have emerged as well. Many Holocaust sites have become places of remembrance and education. Laws have been passed and special courts created so that perpetrators of genocide can be brought to justice. Organizations work to investigate and expose human rights abuses. Holocaust scholar Yehudah Bauer summed up what many consider to be the main lessons of the Holocaust: "Thou shall not be a perpetrator, thou shall not be a victim, and thou shall never, but never, be a bystander." If each person practiced these lessons, it could help to ensure that more genocides would not happen.

May 8, 1945

Germany surrenders,
ending the war in Europe

Nuremberg trials
of the Nazis

**November 1945–
October 1946**

The Yad Vashem
Holocaust museum in
Israel is established

1958

Holocaust
miniseries airs in
West Germany

1953

Elie Wiesel's book
Night is published

1979

Three lawsuits are filed
in New York on behalf
of Holocaust victims and
their families

2005

1996

A Holocaust memorial
is dedicated in
Berlin, Germany

Timeline

December 9, 1948

The United Nations adopts the Convention on the Prevention and Punishment of the Crime of Genocide

Israel declares its independence

May 14, 1948

1949

Germany adopts a constitution that forbids discrimination based on race

1987

The Anti-Defamation League announces the first Courage to Care awards

The United States Holocaust Memorial Museum in Washington, D.C., opens

April 22, 1993

The United Nations establishes the Human Rights Council

2006

2010

World War II museum opens in a Krakow, Poland, factory once owned by Oskar Schindler

Glossary

accreditation—process of giving official approval

annex—addition to a building

annuities—agreements providing for yearly payments

bigotry—strong and unreasonable dislike for a group of people, especially because of their race, nationality, or religion

clemency—reduction of the severity of punishment

conspiracy—secret plot

cremated—burned a dead body

crematory—furnace used for burning dead bodies

decimated—almost destroyed

degenerate—person who has sunk to a lower moral level than normal

deportation—sending people to another country against their will

due process—course of formal proceedings carried out with established rules

indicted—charged with a crime or offense

militias—groups of citizens having some military training that are called into service during emergencies

nonbinding—does not require an action

perpetrators—people who carry out a crime or other offense

plight—difficult or dangerous situation

prematurely—happening before the usual or expected time

propaganda—information spread to try to influence the thinking of people; often not completely true or fair

reparations—money paid to countries for their economic losses

Additional Resources

Further Reading

Boraks-Nemetz, Lilian, and Irene N. Watts, compilers. *Tapestry of Hope: Holocaust Writing for Young People*. Plattsburgh, N.Y.: Tundra Books of Northern New York, 2003.

Frank, Anne. *The Diary of a Young Girl*. New York: Alfred A. Knopf, 2010.

Haugen, Brenda. *The Holocaust Museum*. Minneapolis: Compass Point Books, 2008.

January, Brendan. *Genocide: Modern Crimes Against Humanity*. Minneapolis: Twenty-First Century Books, 2007.

Schroeder, Peter W. *Six Million Paper Clips: The Making of a Children's Holocaust Memorial*. Minneapolis: Kar-Ben Publishing, 2004.

Senker, Cath. *Surviving the Holocaust*. Chicago: Raintree, 2006.

Internet Sites

Use FactHound to find Internet sites related to this book. All of the sites on FactHound have been researched by our staff.

Here's all you do:
Visit *www.facthound.com*
Type in this code: 9780756543938

Select Bibliography

Bazyler, Michael J. *Holocaust Justice: The Battle for Restitution in America's Courts*. New York: New York University Press, 2003.

Berenbaum, Michael. *The World Must Know: The History of the Holocaust as Told in the United States Holocaust Memorial Museum*. Boston: Little, Brown, 1993.

Berger, Joseph. "God Said Multiply, and Did She Ever." 18 Feb. 2010. 10 Aug. 2010. *The New York Times*. www.nytimes.com/2010/02/21/nyregion/21yitta.html?hp

Chartock, Roselle K., and Jack Spencer, eds. *Can It Happen Again? Chronicles of the Holocaust*. New York: Black Dog & Leventhal Paperbacks, 2001.

"Darfur: UN Chief Renews Call on All Parties to Return to Peace Talks." 9 Aug. 2010. 10 Aug. 2010. UN News Centre. www.un.org/apps/news/story.asp?NewsID=35569&Cr=&Cr1=

Dwork, Debórah, and Robert Jan van Pelt. *Holocaust: A History*. New York: Norton, 2002.

Gigliotti, Simone, and Berel Lang, eds. *The Holocaust: A Reader*. Malden, Mass.: Blackwell Publishing, 2005.

Guttenplan, D.D. *The Holocaust on Trial*. New York: W.W. Norton & Co. Inc., 2001.

Lewin, Rhoda G., ed. *Witness to the Holocaust: An Oral History*. New York: Twayne Publishers, 1990.

Smith, Lyn. *Remembering: Voices of the Holocaust*. New York: Carroll & Graf, 2006.

The United States Holocaust Memorial Museum. 10 Aug. 2010. www.ushmm.org/

Yad Vashem. 10 Aug. 2010. www.yadvashem.org/

Source Notes

Chapter 1: Lyn Smith. *Remembering: Voices of the Holocaust*. New York: Carroll & Graf, 2006, p. 286.

Chapter 2: Rhoda G. Lewin, ed. *Witness to the Holocaust: An Oral History*. New York: Twayne Publishers, 1990, p. 107.

Chapter 3: Debórah Dwork and Robert Jan van Pelt. *Holocaust: A History*. New York: Norton, 2002, p. 379.

Chapter 4: Michael Berenbaum. *The World Must Know: The History of the Holocaust as Told in the United States Holocaust Memorial Museum*. Washington: The United States Holocaust Museum, 2006, p. 222.

Chapter 5: *Witness to the Holocaust: An Oral History*, p. 79.

About the Author

Jason Skog has written several books for young readers. He is a freelance writer and former newspaper reporter living in Brooklyn, New York, with his wife and two young sons.

Index